A Call
to
DISCIPLESHIP

By
Susan J. Heck

A Call to Discipleship
By Susan J. Heck

Copyright © 2012
Focus Publishing, Bemidji, Minnesota
All Rights Reserved

Scripture taken from
The New King James Version®
Copyright © 1982
By Thomas Nelson, Inc.
Used by permission
All rights reserved

Cover design by Melanie Schmidt

ISBN 978-1-936141-09-08

Printed in the United States of America

To my dear friend and mentor,
Carolyn Gatewood,
who has taught me much
by her example.

Table of Contents

Chapter One

What is Discipleship?

Many years ago when my husband started a church in Tulsa, Oklah`oma, I was determined that by God's grace and help we would begin a discipling ministry for women. I had such a burden for what I saw as a command to older women in Titus 2, and yet it was not being fulfilled in most churches. I wondered why this ministry was so terribly neglected in the church of Jesus Christ. My heart yearned for this ministry, not only because it was a command by God that was being disobeyed, but also because I saw the results of it in my own life in a negative way when I was a young woman. I was 19 years old when I got married, and 23 years of age when my husband took his first pastorate. I didn't have a clue about being a wife, much less a pastor's wife, at that young age. Many times I longed for an older woman to confide in and help me with the struggles I was having, but I didn't know where to turn or who to turn to. I made a lot of mistakes that I deeply regret and wonder, "Would my life have taken a different direction back then, if some older woman had taken me under her wing and helped me?" "Would I have been a better wife, a better mother, a godlier woman?" And so, as a result of the burden God placed within my heart, our church began this ministry.

I am grateful to say that as a result of this ministry, many lives have been transformed. I am thankful that I now have several older women who invest in my life, and I have been blessed as God has used them in tremendous ways. We also have seen some of the greatest life changes in the women in our church as a result of this ministry. One young woman told me that the discipling relationship has enriched her life both spiritually and emotionally, and that she could not imagine ever being without the woman who is her spiritual mother, her confidante, and her friend.

Not only is it life-changing for the younger women, but this ministry has enriched the lives of the older women as well. In fact, one these ladies told me, "Discipling younger women has been the most fulfilling thing I have ever done." Even the husbands have expressed gratitude for this ministry. The husband of one woman I was discipling called me one day and told me he had a new wife! This was the result of the change that had been made in her life by being discipled. The discipling relationships have helped entire families, and are a positive influence on the church family as well.

With that in mind, I want to give you an outline of where we will be going in this booklet. In this first chapter, we will answer the questions:

- What is Discipleship?
- Why Should We Disciple?
- Who Should Disciple?
- Who Do We Disciple?

In the second chapter, we will answer the question:

- What Do We Teach to the Disciple?

And in the final chapter, chapter three, we will answer the questions:

- When Do We Disciple?
- Where Do We Disciple?
- How Do We Disciple?

What is Discipleship?

And Jesus came and spoke to them, saying, "All authority has been given to Me in heaven and on earth. Go therefore and make disciples of all the nations, baptizing them in the name of the Father and of the Son and of the Holy Spirit, teaching them to observe all things that I have commanded you; and lo, I am with you always, even to the end of the age." Amen (Matthew 28:18-20).

The context in which this verse is spoken by Christ is after His death and resurrection and just before His accession into heaven. These were some of the last words He spoke to His disciples while on earth, so you know they are important. Jesus says that we are to go and make disciples of all nations. The Greek word here for *teach*, or *make disciples*, is *mathetes*. The idea is that of a person who attaches himself or herself to a master with a commitment to follow his teaching and imitate his life. A *disciple* is a learner; he or she is the one who receives instruction. In New Testament times, this was someone who studied and learned according to a set plan, with a view to obey what their master or mentor taught or commanded. This instruction would be both formal and informal, as the student would learn by oral questions and answers, along with memorization, which was the primary way of learning. (This is a lost art in our culture—but that's a topic for another time.)

Jesus, Himself, when training His 12 disciples, instructed them formally, as He did in the Sermon the Mount and the Olivet Discourse. But He also instructed His disciples informally, like the time when He calmed the storm that arose while he was asleep in a boat with his disciples (see Matthew 14), as well as the many healings and miracles He performed, such as the feedings of the 5000 and the 4000. (There are many other accounts in the gospels of these types of happenings.) Jesus utilized these teachable moments to train His disciples. New Testament discipleship is radically different than our modern-day contemporary models.

This same idea was also emphasized by the Apostle Paul in several passages. In 1 Corinthians 4:16, he writes, **"Therefore I urge you, imitate me."** And in 1 Corinthians 11:1, he says, **"Imitate me, just as I also imitate Christ."** And finally, in 2 Thessalonians 3:7-9, we read: **"For you yourselves know how you ought to follow us, for we were not disorderly among you. nor did we eat anyone's bread free of charge, but worked with labor and toil night and day, that we might not be a burden to any of you, not because we do not have authority, but to make ourselves an example of how you should follow us."** We might say discipleship is "you follow me as I follow Christ." It is a high calling indeed, as it indicates that the discipler must have a life that is worthy of emulating, and we will discuss that more in the pages to follow.

Notice that, according to Jesus' words in Matthew 28, there are three elements involved in discipleship. First of all, is the act of *going*. Jesus says *go*. The idea here in the Greek is that as we go through life we are commissioned by God to look for opportunities to disciple others. We look for opportunities to press men and women concerning the issues of the gospel and to repent from their sins and turn to Christ. This is not an option for us, since the Lord commands it.

The second element involved is *baptism*. Now you might say, "Wait a minute! You're not going to tell me that I should go around baptizing people, are you?" Let me explain what Jesus is saying here. In New Testament times, when people would surrender their lives to the Lordship of Christ, they were immediately baptized. Baptism was not something that was put off, as we see today in our evangelical churches. Peter said in Acts 2:38, **"Repent, and let every one of you be baptized in the name of Jesus Christ for the remission of sins; and you shall receive the gift of the Holy Spirit."** And in verse 41 it says, **"Then those who gladly received his word were baptized; and that day about three thousand souls were added to them."** And in Acts 8:12, when Philip was preaching, the same thing occurred—men and women believed and were baptized: **"But when they believed Philip as he preached the things concerning the kingdom of God and the name of Jesus Christ, both men and women were baptized."**

There are many other references that we would do well to study—verses such as Acts 8:38, where Philip was speaking with the Ethiopian eunuch as he was searching the Scriptures. The text tells us he believed and was baptized. Cornelius is another example in Acts 10:47; he also believed and was baptized. Acts 16:15 states that after Lydia believed, she and her household were baptized. The keeper of the prison, in Acts 16:31, when Paul and Silas were miraculously let loose—Paul preached to him, and it states in verses 31-33, that he and his family believed and were baptized. The point is that once we look for opportunities to compel others to surrender their life to the Lordship of Christ, then we also compel them to be baptized. Baptism is a declaration that one is now a disciple of Jesus Christ and involved in a commitment to the Lord. This is really not an option given to a person being evangelized. This is usually one of the first areas I probe when starting to disciple a woman, as it can be very telling regarding her obedience to Christ.

The third element of discipleship according to the text is *teaching*. And notice what Jesus says we are to teach them: *all things that I have commanded you*. This would include all the words of Christ, but, by implication, the whole of Scripture also. This is a high calling indeed, but not an impossible calling. We must help women along in pursuing a life of obedience to the Lord and to His Word. Paul also provides specific areas that we as women are to teach, in Titus 2, which we will cover in the next chapter.

So we might sum up our first question, *What is discipleship?*, by saying this: Discipleship involves a student and a teacher who come together not just to talk about general issues of life, like decorating the house or gardening or sewing, even though that has a place, but in a relationship where the student attaches himself or herself to the teacher for the purpose of growing towards Christ's likeness. This would include changes in her behavior, her attitude and her thinking. Central to discipleship is change and if change is not taking place, then we need to rethink and reexamine what we are doing. Our goal and motive should be to invest our time in the Kingdom of God and His glory. Discipleship is both a following of Jesus Christ and an imitation of what He would do.

Why Should We Disciple?

It won't take long to answer the second question, because God said it and to me that settles it, period. In Matthew 28 Jesus does not give us an option; it is a command to the disciples and to us throughout the ages. *Go therefore, and make disciples*, and Jesus even ends with *Amen*, or so be it.

But another passage to consider is 2 Timothy 2:1, 2. Notice what Paul tells Timothy. **"You therefore, my son, be strong in the grace that is in Christ Jesus. And the things that you have heard from me among many witnesses, commit these to faithful men who will be able to teach others also."** Notice, once again, that this is a command, not an option. The word here for *commit* has the idea of a sacred deposit or trust. Paul is telling Timothy to pass on the things he had heard from Paul to other men, and notice that it is *faithful men*. You don't want to disciple anyone who is not faithful, who has not made that core commitment to Christ; otherwise you are wasting your time, and it will be a fruitless relationship. It is a wonderful principle Paul spells out here for young Timothy. "Timothy, you disciple others who are faithful, and then they will disciple others who are faithful, and so on and so on." It is a wonderful thing to see a woman in whom you have invested your life begin to disciple others and invest her life in them. Only God knows what fruit has been born because of faithful men and women who have committed themselves to the high calling of disciple making.

The last passage to consider in this section is Titus 2:1-5: **"But as for you, speak the things which are proper for sound doctrine: that the older men be sober, reverent, temperate, sound in faith, in love, in patience; the older women likewise, that they be reverent in behavior, not slanderers, not given to much wine, teachers of good things—that they admonish the young women to love their husbands, to love their children, to be discreet, chaste, homemakers, good, obedient to their own husbands, that**

the word of God may not be blasphemed." Again, notice that Paul gives this as a command and not an option. Older men are to teach younger men, and older women are to teach younger women. The word here for *teach* means to school or train.

Now, you might be an older woman, and you might be saying to yourself, "Why should I do this? I have raised my children and now I am free at last. I can do all the things I've been waiting to do and more." Maybe you are a younger woman and you're saying, "No thanks, I don't need any help. I certainly don't want anybody knowing the struggles I have with sin. I am fine just the way I am thank you very much." Both of these attitudes are wrong and sinful, as Paul says this is not an option; it is a command. We, as women, should be actively involved in this mandate. But Paul also gives us another motivating factor for discipling at the end of verse 5, where he states *that the word of God will not be blasphemed.* This means so that the word of God will not be injuriously spoken of. The ungodly world is watching us and they know that we as Christian women are to be different. When the lost world sees us being sober-minded, loving our husbands and our children, being chaste, homemakers, good, and obedient to our own husbands, they take notice. It is a stark contrast to the rest of the world that is so involved in self-indulgent living. When we fail to heed what is admonished here in Titus 2, as well as 2 Timothy and Matthew 28, we bring shame on God's name and God's Word. We hurt the cause of Christ and blaspheme His Word, as Paul says. So the answer to our second question, *Why Should We Disciple?* is a two-fold answer:

1. It is a command by God.
2. So that God's name will not be blasphemed.

Who Should Disciple?

It is hard to get away from the fact that all believers should be involved in this mandate. Jesus doesn't give any qualifiers in Matthew 28; He just gives it as a command to all believers in Christ. The same command is assumed in 2 Timothy 2:2, when Paul tells Timothy to commit what he has learned from him to faithful men. Whether we think we are or not, we all are involved in discipleship right now. Since discipling is "follow me as I follow Christ," we must realize that we are all setting examples to someone. Someone is following us. It could be our children, our grandchildren, our friends, or our family. They are following us and they will mimic us. Some of us may be setting ungodly examples by what we say or do and those that are following us are learning by our example. I remember a time I was visiting in a home with several other people. A child who was present demonstrated terrible disrespect to her father by her tone of voice and attitude of disobedience. An older woman standing nearby took the child by the arm and told her how wicked her behavior was and that she never wanted her to do that again, to which the child replied, "Well, Mommie does it." I thought, "What a terrible indictment on this young mother." I trust that all of us are setting godly, holy examples by our speech and our deeds. (And even our thought life, which no one sees but God.) Sometimes I listen to my children talk or see them do something, and even though they are grown now, they remind me of me. And that can be a scary thing!

In the remainder of this chapter, I want to focus on our role as women. With that in mind, I would like to look more carefully at what Paul specifically says in Titus 2 about who should be discipling or teaching. First of all, he says in verse 3 it is the *older women*. If you think about it, we can all be teaching someone who is younger. Unfortunately, we live in an age where we put older women on shelves, thinking they have nothing to offer younger women. But how wrong we are! With age come experience, wisdom, and the secrets of godly living. Older women can save the younger women a lot of grief and heartache. One of the things I have looked forward to as I age is to be actively involved in this ministry. It has truly been the joy of my heart. This word could also mean that she is older in the Lord. In other words, she has more spiritual maturity than the woman she disciples. In our church, the women who are involved in discipling younger women have grown children, or children who are in junior high or high school. It is probably not a wise thing to put a young woman with pre-school children in this position, as she has neither the wisdom nor the experience to handle teaching someone much older than she is. The younger woman's main role should be discipling her children and pouring her life into them. This does not exclude her from fulfilling the great commission to go and make disciples, however, for it is good for younger women to invest their lives in young people. I am very grateful for the men and the women who invested in my children when they were teenagers and still living at home. It was a huge blessing, as many times they could impact my children in a way that their father and I could not.

Notice that Paul gives Titus four elements that should be characteristic of these older women who are involved in teaching or discipling younger women:

1. She must be reverent in her behavior. In the Greek this means behavior that is becoming as a priest. She must be a holy woman or a priestess, we might say. She must have a godly, separated life. We would not want an ungodly woman instructing a younger woman.

2. She must not be a slanderer. This means that she should not be involved in gossip or slander. John Calvin once said, "Talkativeness is a disease of women and it gets worse with age." Again, you would not want to give a woman who is a gossip the job of discipling a younger woman, as she may pass that wicked sin on to the one she mentors. Also, it would create a question of trust between the two women.

3. She is not to be given to much wine. You might be thinking, "Say what?" We need to remember that Paul wrote this book to Titus, who was ministering on the isle of Crete. Now the isle of Crete was not a wonderful place to minister, as it was a place full of wickedness. We would not call it the "Bible Belt"—that is for sure! "Sinner's Square" might be a better name for Crete. In fact, consider what Paul writes about this place in Titus 1:12-13: **"One of them, a prophet of their own, said, 'Cretans are always liars, evil beasts, lazy gluttons.' This testimony is true. Therefore rebuke them sharply, that they may be sound in the faith."** The Cretans were known as liars and they were a people who were unrestrained in their passions and consumed by their appetites. Drunkenness was a problem on the isle of Crete, and so Paul tells Titus that these older women should not be enslaved to much wine. I would draw a principle here and say that any woman who is enslaved to any sin that she is not actively trying to fight against would be wise not to engage in training younger women, as many times the younger woman will mimic that same sin pattern. I remember many years ago I was being discipled by an older woman who had the habit of snorting when she laughed. Do you know what I discovered after awhile? I found myself snorting when *I* laughed! Now, snorting is not a sin, but I share this personal example to demonstrate what I am saying. Sinful habits that an older woman has will be mimicked by the person she disciples.

4. She is to be a teacher of good things. Then Paul gives us a list of those good things in verses 4 and 5: **"that they admonish the young women to love their husbands, to love their children, to be discreet, chaste, homemakers, good, obedient to their own husbands, that the word of God may not be blasphemed."** She must have a life worthy of emulating. Some churches have safeguards in place where elders approve the women who will be discipling other women. Others have a women's council that is actively aware of the women who are able to be involved in this ministry. There are many contexts in which we may examine the lives of women in the church and determine who should be discipling. This is for the protection of the church and for the glory of God and His Kingdom, as we do not want to offer Him anything but excellence in ministry. However, other churches have less formal discipling relationships, which are naturally developed. It is always wise to be under the submission of the church leadership as to the direction they want to take this ministry.

Who Should We Disciple?

When we consider this passage in Matthew 28:18-20, we would have to say that the great commission is to disciple all nations. We look for opportunities to compel men and women to embrace the claims of the gospel. With that in mind, we would say that without a person having saving faith it would be impossible to disciple him or her. We might be able to give a lost person some helps that would give them temporary changes, but without the Holy Spirit, it is impossible to make changes that will last. Paul states in 2 Corinthians 5:17, **"Therefore, if anyone is in Christ, he is a new creation; old things have passed away; behold, all things have become new."** The women in whom we invest our lives should have genuine saving faith, that is, they should have a turning away from sin, self and a life of disobedience, with a turning toward righteousness, the Lord, and a life of obedience to God. Again, let me say that we are to evangelize the lost, and many times that might be a woman you disciple.

In 2 Timothy 2:1, 2, Paul tells young Timothy that the men he pours his life into must be faithful. The word here for *faithful* in the Greek means trustworthy or reliable. This is a quality that is necessary in those we disciple if we are going to commit anything to them that will last. One of the things I require from any woman I disciple is that she will commit to the means of grace. By that, I mean that she will be faithful to be in the Word and to fellowship with God through prayer, that she will read through her Bible (hopefully at least once a year), that she will be faithful to assemble with God's people when they assemble, faithful to complete any assignments I give, and faithful to meet with me. If they balk at those requests you can usually bank on an unteachable heart and a rocky discipling relationship. These things should be the basic core commitments of a genuine believer.

Consider Titus 2, where Paul tells Titus, specifically in verse 4, that older woman are to teach or disciple younger women. Now this might be someone younger than you in age, or just someone who is younger in the Lord. Many of the women I have discipled are older than me in physical age, but younger in spiritual age. I have also discipled younger women who I thought should be discipling me. Many times it is a mutual learning process, as Proverbs 27:17 says **"iron sharpens iron."** So when you put these three passages together, the answer to our "who" question would be: faithful women who possess genuine saving faith.

13

You might ask, well how do I know if she really is redeemed? We will endeavor to answer that question in chapter three of this booklet. And we'll also cover some practical things that I think will help you as you think through this important command to disciple young women.

Let's briefly answer our questions from this chapter: *What is Discipleship?* It is a relationship in which a person attaches himself or herself to a master with a commitment to follow their teaching and imitate their life. You follow me as I follow Christ. *Why Should We Disciple?* First, because it is a command by God; and second, specifically for us as women, so that the Word of God will not be dishonored. *Who Should Disciple?* All believers are commanded to disciple. However, older women are specifically singled out and commanded to teach young women. *Who Do We Disciple?* Faithful women who possess genuine saving faith.

As we close this chapter, I want to get a little personal. The question that is foremost on my mind is this: are *you* a disciple of Jesus Christ? I would be doing a disservice to my Lord if I failed to compel you to commit your life to His Lordship. What I mean by that is: Has there been a time in your life when you repented of your sin and turned your life over to Christ's Lordship? Are you now following Him by obeying Him? We cannot disciple someone else if we ourselves are not a disciple of Christ.

Another question I would like for you to consider is this: Are you under the myth that discipling is for someone else, but not for you? It is hard to get away from the command of our Lord to go and make disciples. This is not an option for us. It is a command. Maybe we should remind ourselves of what John says in 1 John 2:3-4, **"Now by this we know**

that we know Him, if we keep His commandments. He who says, 'I know Him,' and does not keep His commandments, is a liar, and the truth is not in him." I would encourage you as older women to consider the high calling as well as the high privilege that we have to disciple women. I would encourage you to invest your time in things that count for eternity, and not to waste your life on things that are temporal. To be able to pass on to someone else the wisdom God has given you, along with your experience in life, is a valuable gift to a younger woman. It is worth more than material possessions. Also, to be able to stand before the Lord someday and hear, "Well done, good and faithful servant," will be a joy beyond any earthly accomplishment.

If you are a younger woman reading this booklet, I must ask you "Are you willing to allow another woman to invest in your life?" Is pride keeping you from saying "I need help"? Dear one, please don't make the same mistake I made as a young mother with small children. I deeply regret those wasted years and there is nothing I can do about them now. I have seen young women who desperately need the help of an older woman and yet they refuse—which is a warning sign to me. I see them heading down paths of destruction and it grieves me!

For those of you who are already involved in this wonderful mandate of discipling others: good for you! I rejoice with you! I would ask you to evaluate your own personal walk with God, and ask yourself these questions: Does my life reflect behavior that is holy? Am I a gossip? ·Am I enslaved to *any* sin? Am I passing on good things to those I teach? Do I have a life worth emulating? Would anyone want to follow me as I follow Christ?

In the next chapters we'll discover what we are to teach to our disciples, as well as when, where and how to disciple. I will also share with you some books and helps that I have found most valuable in this ministry of discipling women. It is my deepest desire for all of you that with God's help you, yourself, will be a Titus 2 woman, and then take that challenge and pass it on to a younger woman!

Chapter Two
What Do We Teach to the Disciple?

When I got married I was 19 years old. I was under the same myth that most young women are today, that is, that my husband and I would have a perfect marriage. Everything would be "peachy cream" and we "would live happily ever after." We would never argue and life would be perfect. WRONG! Not too long after we were married I realized everything was not "peachy cream," but more like "rocky road." Live happily ever after? NOT! He would be lucky to live at all. Our first few years were an adjustment indeed. As I mentioned in the previous chapter, I needed an older woman to come alongside and help me with my struggles. And one of my struggles was in the area of submission. I did not have a clue as to what it meant, and I was not going to have anybody telling me what to do. I had an erroneous idea about submission, and because of my rebellious attitude I created a myriad of problems. I remember when God saved me at the age of 30 and I began to study what submission really was, and then began obeying God in this area, that my marriage became much easier. I began to see submission as freeing and not as binding. I became liberated in a real sense. With submission in mind, I want to move right on to our next question:

What Do We Teach to the Disciple?

People often ask me about the discipling ministry at our church, and one of the questions is, "What curriculum do you use?" The exciting thing is that even though there is some good stuff out there, Paul tells us here in Titus 2 what we are to teach. The curriculum Paul gives in Titus 2 is a seven-fold curriculum. Now, I will share some things that I have found to be helpful, but I will caution you by saying that there is some very dangerous stuff out there, too. So please be careful as you choose material to aid you in the discipling process. You want to make sure the books you use outside of the Bible are biblically and doctrinally sound. Let's remind ourselves again of the passage in Titus 2 before we get into the seven-fold curriculum.

> **... the older women likewise, that they be reverent in behavior, not slanderers, not given to much wine, teachers of good things—that they admonish the young women to love their husbands, to love their children, to be discreet, chaste, homemakers, good, obedient to their own husbands, that the word of God may not be blasphemed. (Titus 2:3-5 NKJV)**

Now, because I often teach from the King James Version, and will refer to the terms used in that version, I've included that version's rendering for your benefit, since it differs somewhat from the New King James Version.

> **... that they may teach the young women to be sober, to love their husbands, to love their children, to be discreet, chaste, keepers at home, good, obedient to their own husbands, that the word of God be not blasphemed. (Titus 2:4-5 KJV)**

The first thing in Paul's curriculum of what an older woman is to teach to a younger woman is to be *sober*, or sober-minded. (This also is the same Greek word used for discreet.) You might say, "Does this mean I teach her not to get drunk?" Well, that would be a good idea, but that is not what this word means. The Greek word for sober is *sophron*, and it means to be of sound mind, self-controlled, and to limit one's freedoms. This is a woman who exercises self-control with proper restraints on all her passions and desires. Someone once said it means to bring her to her senses, to wise her up to her wifely duties. Younger women need to be taught to be serious, to be sensible and to use good judgment. They need to keep their passion under control! I remember as a young woman that I needed help in getting my emotions under control. There were times my poor husband couldn't even look at me a certain way without tears flowing. I also remember getting angry at him for the most ridiculous things. One particular incident happened soon after we were married. He told me he did not like the tacos I had fixed for dinner and I did not speak to him for three days! I certainly was not behaving as a woman with her emotions under control. I needed to be brought under control by an older woman who would invest her life in me and help me with this sinful attitude.

This self-control would not only include her emotions, but also her physical passions, perhaps her sexual appetite or physical appetite. Her speech may also need to be brought under control. This is one area in which all women need help. Gossip, slander, angry words should be dealt with and rooted out. James says in chapter 3, verse 8 of his epistle that our tongues are **"an unruly evil, full of deadly poison,"** and that no man came tame it. We need to train young women to speak words that are edifying, words that are lovely, words that are true, and words that are of a good report.

Self-control would also include teaching her to control the financial aspect of her life. Some young woman will not control their compulsive spending habits and they need to be brought under control. A woman who is sober-minded, for example, will not purchase items she knows she cannot afford. She will live within the means God has provided. I am convinced many women are working today just because they refuse to live within the means of their husband's salary.

A woman who is sober will also get her thought life under control. She will not let her mind go out of control with unrealistic or hysterical thoughts. I remember as a young wife and mother that there were times my husband or my children were late in getting home and in my mind I had them in a traffic accident and dead. I would let my mind go out of control with ridiculous thoughts to the point of having their funeral planned. All those "what ifs" are useless thinking, and show a mind that is out of control. We must stop and think, "What are we thinking?" We need to train young women to replace useless thoughts with God-honoring thoughts. Instead of thinking, "My husband is late; he must be dead or in a traffic accident," we can think, "My husband is late; yes, that is true. He could be in a traffic jam, or he might have stopped at the store to buy me some flowers. Or you know, even if he is dead or in a horrible traffic accident, God will give me the grace to deal with it." We need to train women to renew their minds and thoughts with the Word of God. They should memorize His truths and meditate on them day and night. (One of the many reasons I am a big advocate of Scripture memorization is because I have seen changes in the way women think who have taken the challenge to memorize the Word and allow the Word of God to renew their thinking.) Many times a husband may not be able to reach a resisting wife, but a godly older woman can come alongside and help her restrain these out-of-control passions.

The second area we are to pass on to the women we disciple is teaching them how to *love their husbands*. Now to understand this point, we must understand the times in which Titus was written. In Biblical times marriages were arranged, and a young bride would be forced to live with and love a man who would very likely be a total stranger. She would need an older woman who had already been through this and could help her learn how to love her husband. But ladies, even in a culture where we marry for "love," we must admit that loving one's husband can be a challenge at times. The Greek word for *love* here is *phileo*. It conveys the idea of cherishing the object above all else, showing tender affection characterized by constancy.

I remember when I fell in love with my husband that all I could do was think about Doug Heck. I was crazy about him. I wanted to be with him all the time and do things for him that would manifest my love. That is *phileo* love. You can be around some women and it seems that they get some kind of pleasure out of criticizing their husbands and dishonoring them. It is very grievous sin against God. They seem to enjoy complaining that he doesn't take the trash out, he doesn't spend enough time with the kids, he doesn't do this or that … drip, drip, drip, like a leaky faucet. This is not a woman who shows love to her husband. We need to come alongside these young women and teach them how to love their husbands and to teach them that this is a privilege, not a burden. We must disciple them in how to show love to their husbands physically, emotionally, and spiritually. We need to teach them the importance of taking time to listen to their husbands, even when what they are talking about doesn't interest them. We need to train them to warmly greet their husbands at the end of the day, even when they have perhaps had a lousy day. And along with that, we teach them not to greet him at the door with a list of all the things that went wrong during the day before he can even say hello! Instead, our focus should be on what he does do, not what he doesn't do. We should be grateful that we even have a husband.

The third quality that should be passed down to young women is that of *loving her children*. Now again, think biblically with me. These women would have arranged marriages with men that perhaps they would not be too fond of, and then along came children from that union and she may have difficulty loving those children. So, she would need to learn to love her children. But nothing is new under the sun, right? Today, loving one's children can sometimes be equally as hard. Let's face it—sometimes they are not so lovely. Sometimes we as moms have a hard time not favoring one child over another. Sometimes a child with a difficult disability or one who is rebellious is hard to love. And yet the command is to love our children. The word for love here is *phileo*, which is the same love we are to show our husbands. Loving our children is shown by cherishing our children and having affection toward them which is to be consistent. What are some of the best ways to show love to our children and to teach young women to love their children? In Ephesians 6:4 Paul gives us two of the best ways to show love to our children. Paul says, **"And you, fathers, do not provoke your children to wrath, but bring them up in the training and admonition of the Lord."** The King James Version says nurture and admonition of the Lord. What does this mean exactly? To *nurture* would entail the discipline, and the *admonition* would involve words of encouragement.

Let's take the nurturing first, in the discipline of children, which is an evidence of a parent's love for the child. I guess this is one of the areas that grieves me as I disciple women. I see them refusing to do what God says regarding disciplining their children. What hardships they bring on themselves. Parenting is not hard if you will do it God's way. Proverbs 22:15 says, **"Foolishness is bound up in the heart of a child; the rod of correction will drive it far from him."** Proverbs 23:13 says, **"Do not withhold correction from a child, for if you beat him with a rod, he will not die."** Let me tell you ladies, I had a father who believed in discipline and I am not dead! And neither are my other six siblings! Proverbs 29:15 tells us, **"The rod and rebuke give wisdom, but a child left to himself brings shame to his mother."** I don't know about you but that's the way I feel when I see a child out of control at the grocery store, the mall or any other public place. It's not the poor child who is to blame; it is the parents. If parents don't discipline their children, then you have to ask, "Do they really love them?"

In Hebrews 12:6 we have an interesting verse that tell us that our Heavenly Father disciplines those who are His because He loves them: **"For whom the LORD loves He chastens, and scourges every son whom He receives."** The writer of Hebrews goes on to say in verse 8, **"But if you are without chastening, of which all have become partakers, then you are illegitimate and not sons."** Ladies, the Lord loves us enough to discipline us and if we are not experiencing His discipline, then it proves that we are not His children. If you are discipling a young woman and she does not discipline her children, then it is in serious question whether she loves them or not.

Paul mentions the second way in which we love our children in Ephesians 6:4, and that is through *admonition*. This means by words of encouragement. The most encouraging words that mothers can give their children are the Words of God. We should train and encourage our children in spiritual things, teaching them biblical principles. We should do that when we sit and when we walk and when we lie down and rise up, as Deuteronomy 6:7 states. We need to be there to listen to their problems and to answer their questions. We should pray with them and for them. We must show them affection and tell them we love them. These are all ways we can show love and encouragement to our children. We must not tear them down by yelling at them and calling them unkind names. For those of you who have grown children, you know what I mean when I say the time slips by too fast. When I was a young mother, I used to think people who said that were foolish, but now that I am on the other side, I say true, true, true! Those years can never be reclaimed. There are enough children in this world who are unloved, and we need to instruct young woman to be different, to love their children.

The fourth area of instruction in our discipling curriculum is to teach young women to be *chaste* as seen in verse 5. This means to be pure in their heart and in their life. It also includes being free from defilement. The isle of Crete, as I mentioned earlier, was especially known for their ungodliness, and so the older women needed to come alongside the younger women and teach them how to be pure. Oh, how needed this is in our day as well! Our world is filled with so much immorality, unholiness and impurity. We need to teach the younger women how to avoid impure things, to walk within their house with a perfect heart and to set no wicked things before their eyes, as the Psalmist says in Psalm 101. Paul says in 1 Thessalonians 4:7, **"... for God did not call us to uncleanness, but in holiness."** A lot of young women get hooked on soap operas, trashy novels, unwholesome magazines, music with lyrics that tell them they aren't appreciated, and pornography, which is readily available on the internet, and the results are disastrous. They say the average woman watches 30 hours of television per week. First of all, I am curious to know where they get that kind of time; and secondly, what on earth is on television that is worth 30 hours of their time? It is sad to say that many of us know what's on television for the week, but we don't know where the simplest things are in the Bible. Young women also need instruction in how to be pure in their speech, their time, their thought life, and even in choosing right friends. Paul says in 1 Corinthians 15:33, **"Do not be deceived: 'Evil company corrupts good habits.'"** I have seen women spiral downward in their walk with God just because they have chosen the wrong friends with whom to spend the bulk of their time.

The fifth thing on our curriculum is to teach young women to be *keepers at home*. Now before you cast stones at me, remember that *I* did not say it—*God* said it. I know this is a very controversial subject, especially in our feminist society, but nonetheless we cannot disregard the Word of God. The word here for *keepers at home* comes from two Greek words, which together mean housekeeper. This is a woman who looks after the domestic concerns of the house, as well as her duties to the family. She is the woman mentioned in Proverb 31:27, where it says about her: **"She watches over the ways of her household, and does not eat the bread of idleness."**

Our first duty should be to our home. Unfortunately, our society seems to look down on women who stay at home, as if we have some sort of plague. They fail to understand that many of us see this role as a high calling from our Lord. To be able to rear children to the glory of God and to invest in eternal matters instead of things that are going to burn up someday is a godly goal for women. I know that when I was a young mother, I worked for a very brief period of time, and it took its toll on my spiritual life as well as my family life. Since that time, I have not had to work outside the home, and I am indeed thankful to God for that. Now I know that there are circumstances which are perhaps unavoidable, but the ideal, especially while the children are in the home, is to be at home. Sometimes, the problem is the wife who will not live within the means that God has provided for her. Many times, when there is an unusual financial need in a family there is the option of working from the home. I know both my daughter and daughter-in-law have work they do from the home to supplement their husbands' income. This enables them both to take care of their home and their children and be industrious at the same time. Again, Proverbs 31 mentions this as an attribute of a virtuous woman: **"She considers a field and buys it; from her profits she plants a vineyard"** (Proverb 31:16).

While we are on the subject of teaching women to be keepers at home, I would like to bring out that just because a woman is at home does not mean she is necessarily a keeper at home, if you know what I mean. Our homes should be cleaned and organized and not look like a tornado has gone through them. I have seen some women's homes who "stay at home" and their homes look like they sit all day eating bon-bons and watching television or surfing the net. We need to train women how to clean their house, how to organize things, how to cook, how to plan a menu, how to grocery shop, and how to be hospitable. Some young moms don't have a clue about fixing healthy meals, or how to provide a peaceful and happy environment, or how to manage their time. All of these things would fall under the category of teaching women to be keepers at home.

The sixth quality that we must pass down to younger woman as we disciple them is *goodness*. Paul says we are to teach them to be *good*. This word means to be benevolent, profitable or useful, and the good is to benefit others. This reminds me of the woman again mentioned in Proverbs 31, where is says in verse 20 that **"she extends her hand to the poor, Yes, she reaches out her hands to the needy."** We need to teach young women to see needs in her immediate family, her church family and in her neighborhood. And then we need to teach her how to extend her hand to be beneficial to others. We need to teach her how to sacrifice her time and energy and maybe even her resources to benefit someone else. We need to teach young women to live for others and show her practical ways to do that. We have become a very selfish, isolated society and we need to teach young women to look out for the interests and needs of others.

The last area in our curriculum is the dreaded (for some) "S" word—submission! This is number seven on Paul's list of things in which we should be training young women. Notice what Paul says: *obedient to their own husbands*. Remember again, *I* did not say it; *God* said it. In our culture, which has become increasingly focused on self and one's rights, we have to fight hard against the attitude which says, "No one is going to tell me what to do." We need to come alongside the younger women and teach them to be submissive. The Greek word here is to place in an orderly fashion under. We might say the husband is a five-star general and the wife is a four-star general, or the husband is the president and the wife is the vice-president. This word is also used in Ephesians 5:22 and 23, where Paul says, **"Wives, submit to your own husbands, as to the Lord. For the husband is head of the wife, as also Christ is head of the church; and He is the Savior of the body."** Paul gives us the reason why it is so important that we teach women to submit to their husbands. The husband and wife relationship is to represent Christ and the church. Christ is the head of the church, just as the husband is the head of the wife.

Also, in Colossians 3:18 Paul says, **"Wives, submit to your own husbands, as is fitting in the Lord."** And in 1 Peter 3:1 Peter tells wives they must be subject even to their unsaved husbands: **"Wives, likewise, be submissive to your own husbands, that even if some do not obey the word, they, without a word, may be won by the conduct of their wives."** Now ladies, this does mean that a woman is a doormat, or that she can never express an opinion or an idea. But it does mean she lets her husband make the final decisions in the family. I know this is a hard one for us as women, even for those of us who are older. The reason it is so hard is that it is a part of the curse that we inherited from our mother, Eve, and something we will always fight against because of our sinful flesh. When Adam and Eve sinned they each got cursed for their disobedience. The woman's curse was two-fold. Genesis 3:16 says, **"To the woman He said: 'I will greatly multiply your sorrow and your conception; in pain you shall bring forth children; your desire shall be for your husband, and he shall rule over you.'"** God told Eve that her desire would be to rule over Adam, but that he would rule over her!

As I said, it took me a long time to learn that submission was indeed a blessing and very liberating. I am just sorry that it took me so long to learn it. Women need help to understand how to let their husband wear the pants in the family and how to do it graciously, not giving him the silent treatment for days when they don't agree. They need instruction in how to make gracious appeals when they disagree. You might hear from a younger woman, "Well, if my husband loved me the way Christ loves the church, then submission would be a piece of cake." Well, maybe so, but that does not negate our responsibility. I have seen some women make important decisions without consulting their husbands and some go so far as to purposely defy their wishes. This is an awful indictment on the role of the wife, and brings shame to the name of Christ.

Now before we go on, I do want to say that there would be an exception to this command, and that would be if the husband were to ask the wife to do anything that is in direct violation to the Word of God. This is where she would have to graciously decline and obey God over her husband, as the principle is so clearly set forth in Acts 5:29, where Peter and the other apostles were forbidden to share the gospel, which is a direct command from God, and they responded with **"we ought to obey God rather than men."** For example, if her husband asked her to look at pornography with him, a wife would have to decline, as she would have biblical precedent to do so. Ephesians 5:3 is very clear on this: **"But fornication and all uncleanness or covetousness, let it not even be named among you, as is fitting for saints."** Another example would be in the case of an unsaved husband forbidding his wife to go to church. She might ask him which service (Sunday morning, Sunday night, or Wednesday night, for example) he would like her to attend. This would still allow him to be the head of the house, but also allow her to obey Hebrews 10:25, which says: **"not forsaking the assembling of ourselves together, as is the manner of some, but exhorting one another, and so much the more as you see the Day approaching."** Let me add here that this is where an older and wiser woman is so important, because oftentimes a young woman needs help in discerning what is a sin and what is a preference.

So in answer to our question, *What Do We Teach to the Disciple?* we have Paul's seven-fold curriculum. We teach the younger women to be *sober-minded*, to *love their husbands*, to *love their children*, to be *chaste*, to be *keepers at home*, to be *good*, and to be *submissive to their own husbands*. May I also add that this obviously does not mean that these seven things are the only areas in which we disciple. We also mentor women in the whole of Scripture as Jesus said in Matthew 28: 19, 20. This would mean that we who are older women should know what God says and be able to instruct a younger woman in the things of the Lord. This may seem like an impossible task, but it is not with the help of our Lord! Let's turn to chapter three, where we can get into some practical things that will aid us in the Titus 2 mandate.

Chapter Three
When, Where and How Do We Disciple?

Many years ago I was having a discussion with my daughter about my method of discipleship and she said she had been mentored by two women in the past. She said that my method of discipleship, which is mostly formal, was not her preference. She said that the style she preferred was less formal. So, which is true discipleship—formal or informal? Which is best—formal or informal discipleship? We have seen in the first chapter that both are true, and that our Lord used both formal and informal methods of discipling His twelve men. With that in mind, let us now answer the remainder of our questions, which include *When, Where,* and *How Do We Disciple?*

When Do We Disciple?

I usually meet with the ladies I disciple every other week. First of all, it prevents them from becoming dependent on me, which can be a danger in discipling. You want them to depend on the Lord and not on you. Also, if I meet with a woman every other week, instead of every week, it allows me to disciple more women. But I would say if you have a woman who is a new believer, or who is needy or going through a crisis, you might want to start out meeting every week, and then taper off to every other week. A lot of it will depend on her schedule and yours. Meeting with them before or after church is helpful since you're both already there, hopefully. Perhaps, if you can't physically meet often, you can call her, or e-mail her. I have found both the phone and e-mail to be very effective ministry tools.

Where Do We Disciple?

Let's consider the question of where to meet when we disciple. I personally like to meet in their home or mine when possible. If I am in their home, it gives me an opportunity to see if they are a keeper at home, and perhaps also allows me to see them interact with their children or their husbands. Many times I have stopped a discipling session to point out areas I see with a young woman's husband or children. I have even stopped a session to encourage and help a young mother who needs to discipline a misbehaving child. I have been in women's homes when their husbands call and they have been disrespectful on the phone, and so it is a good time for me to point that out and to help them and hold them accountable. It is a great training time. But I also like to have them in my home, which is sometimes a challenge, because my husband studies mainly at home, and he likes to pop in my office right in the middle of our sessions. But as mentioned earlier, we learn by example, and so if they are in my home, then they can see how I react to my husband. They also can see what kind of "keeper at home" I am, and how I respond to every day living.

I also have women I meet in a restaurant or coffee shop, at the church, or at the park. The park is especially nice if they have children. The children can play as we disciple. I have also taken the women I disciple on ministry journeys to the hospital with me or to see the elderly or the widows in our church. We have made cookies together and taken them to various people in our church body. This is good training for them, as they not only need to be discipled in character and doctrine, but in ministry as well. I try to look for extra times to spend with them besides our scheduled times, perhaps having her family over for dinner or taking her on some of my travels when I go out of town and speak. When we look at Christ we see that he mentored the twelve by teaching them, but also by challenging them in ministry, and by example as they would observe Him. So the list is really endless. The key is not to get into a rut but to be creative. Most important, do spend time with them! Discipleship is not necessarily taught, but caught. They will remember not so much what you say, but what you do—just like your children!

How Do We Disciple?

You might be saying, "I can't do all that!" You're right—you can't! Without God you can do nothing! But *with* Him you can do all things. When we look at Matthew 28:18-20, we see that Jesus gives a promise along with the command to go and make disciples. The promise is "Lo, I am with you always!" This is a promise from God to be with us in this discipling process! This is a great comfort and a great joy! We can disciple another woman knowing that we have the promise of God's grace and power. Also, may I say, we do this with a lot of prayer, and a lot of love.

As we think about how to do this, there are some helpful materials, which I would like to recommend for the discipleship process. The best book I have ever read on the subject of the wife is the *Excellent Wife*, by Martha Peace.[1] Martha deals with the role of the wife in a biblical way and she is very thorough. She deals with real stuff—real thoughts

---

1   Martha Peace, *The Excellent Wife* (Bemidji, MN: Focus Publishing, 1999).

and real problems that women have. She has wonderful charts and practical helps! It is a must. There is a study guide that you can also get to go with it. I almost always go through this with the women I disciple. Another book Martha has written is *Becoming a Titus 2 Woman*.[2] This is a great help in aiding the material we have covered in this booklet, as well as a tool to use with the woman you are discipling when you think it is time to "kick her out of the nest!" This helps her to prepare to begin her own discipling. Other helpful books are *Self-Confrontation: A Manual for In-Depth Discipleship*, by John C. Broger.[3] This is an excellent tool in discipleship, especially in helping woman with life-dominating sins like anger, bitterness, depression, fear, worry and much more. It teaches them how to confront these issues and to put them off. It also has wonderful charts and worksheets for your disciple to work on throughout the week.

Another book that is helpful especially if you are working with a woman who struggles with her thought life is *Loving God With All Your Mind*, by Elizabeth George.[4] This is a great tool in helping women to think biblically, especially if they are in a sinful habit of giving way to hysterical thoughts and dwelling on all the "what ifs." Scripture memorization is a *very* effective tool in getting women to think biblically. Most women I disciple memorize Scripture, many memorizing whole books of the Bible. It has changed the way they think and it has revolutionized their lives. For more information about Scripture memorization see *A Call*

---

2   Martha Peace, *Becoming a Titus 2 Woman* (Bemidji, MN: Focus Publishing, 1997).

3   John C. Broger, *Self-Confrontation: A Manuel for In-Depth Discipleship* (Biblical Counseling Foundation, 1991).

4   Elizabeth George, *Loving God With All Your Mind* (Eugene, OR: Harvest House Publishers, 1997).

to Scripture Memory.[5] One last book I would recommend is *Women Helping Women: A Biblical Guide to Major Issues Women Face*, by Carol Cornish and Elyse Fitzpatrick,[6] (There are numerous other women who contributed to this book as well.). This book deals with helping women who are discontent with their singleness, women who have had abortions, women who are teen-age mothers, women who have troubled marriages, women who are married to unbelievers, women with addictions, women who have adopted children, women in menopause and numerous other issues. This book covers just about any problem a woman might have!

These are a few of the resources I use, but there are many more. I would encourage you to make sure that any thing you use outside of the Scriptures are approved by the leadership of your church. There are some very dangerous materials out there labeled "Christian" that are a far cry from Christian.

You might ask, "Well, what do I do the first time I meet with this young gal?" I usually start out by hearing her testimony. This is a must! I have found many times that women think they are redeemed and after hearing their testimony I discover they really do not understand the essentials of the gospel. Having been there myself, this is very, very important. I was so deceived for so many years, and am grateful to God that He showed me my deception and hypocrisy. So if I have a red flag after hearing their testimony, I go over the areas of faith, repentance, and surrender of one's life to the Lordship

---

5   Susan Heck, *A Call to Scripture Memory* (Bemidji, MN: Focus Publishing, 2009).

6   Carol Cornish and Elyse Fitzpatrick, *Women Helping Women: A Biblical Guide to Major Issues Women Face* (Eugene, OR: Harvest House Publishers, 1997).

of Jesus Christ. You can ask self-examination questions like, "Do you have regular fellowship with God and do you enjoy it?" "Do you love God's word?" "Do you obey it?" "Do you confess your sins and repent of them?" "Do you love other believers?" "Do you experience answered prayer?" "Do you look forward to Christ's return?" These and other questions like these are very revealing regarding their heart, and will perhaps reveal an unregenerate heart.

Next, I gather information about her family, the names of her husband and children, and find out if they are redeemed. This will make a difference in how I disciple her. I will then ask questions regarding the seven-fold curriculum in Titus 2. I ask them to rate themselves on a scale of 1-10 on each of the seven areas to see where they are, so I will know how to help them. For example, "On a scale of 1-10, 1 being the worst and 10 being the best, how would you rate yourself on being sober-minded?" Of course, this means I (and you) must know what it means to be sober-minded and might need to probe further by asking questions about her emotional life, her thought life, her spending, etc. I also ask questions such as, "What do you see as a main goal of our time together?" "What is the most difficult trial you are facing right now?" "If I were to ask you what your spiritual temperature is from a level of 1-10 (1 being the lowest, and 10 being the highest) where would you say you are? What keeps you from being a 10? What would God have you do about it?"

You might wonder why I ask so many questions. The reason is that gathering data is so important, because it enables you to know where to go in your time with her. I usually think and pray about the information I have received and then decide what to start working on with her, and how to pray for her. I cannot stress praying enough! Pray before you meet, when you meet and after you meet. I also like to make sure that she is teachable. I have met with some women who are not teachable, and you usually end up spinning your wheels and wasting their time and yours. Sometimes a teachable spirit is not really evident until after you meet a few times and get to know her better.

That brings me to one last thing I do in that first session and that is to stress confidentiality. She is not going to feel free to share anything with you if she thinks you are going to run out and tell your best friend or your husband. I do let her know however, that the only exception to this is when she is in sin and refuses to repent. I then must follow the commands of the Lord in Matthew 18:15-18, where I am commanded if there is no repentance to bring in other witnesses to confront her, and if there is no repentance after that then it is to be told to the church, and then if there is no repentance after the church pursues her, then she is to be excommunicated. Confidentiality without personal accountability is not biblical.

You might say, "Well, is this a life-long deal?" "Am I signing a life-long contract?" Well, yes, discipleship is a life-long deal. But you don't have to sign a life-long contract with one woman. I would hope that you would always be interested in her life, just as you are your children's lives, but I personally have found that about 1-2 years is a good amount of time for discipling an individual. Some I have met with for shorter periods of time, some much, much longer. Each woman is different and you have to discern what each one's needs are. Remember that Jesus met with His disciples for three and a half years. You do want to meet long enough to make sure she has made enough progress to go out and disciple someone else, but at the same time you don't want to create a dependency on you. I usually start with a 3 month commitment, and then I reevaluate often. I never assume that I am that one that brings her one step closer to maturity in Christ Jesus, and so I ask her how she thinks things are going. Also, personalities may not mix, or I may just not be the one to work with her. Perhaps a different woman in the church could get better results with her. Many times a woman will be resistant to change and, when she realizes this is serious stuff and not just chit-chat over coffee, she may flee! In the many years I have been involved in this ministry, I have had several women do that, and it's difficult because I know they need the accountability and I love them, but you cannot force it. Discipling may mean that you need to rethink your schedule. We are a very individualistic and isolated society—but that is not biblical. My husband, Doug, once said, "Hurried schedules, void of relational discipleship and other means of grace, will shrink our soul to tolerate a mediocre ministry and stagnant Christian life."

So, let's sum up everything we have learned:

What is Discipleship? It is the relationship in which a person attaches himself or herself to a master with a commitment to follow their teaching and imitate their life. You follow me as I follow Christ.

Why Should We Disciple? Because it is commanded by God, and specifically for us as women, so that the Word of God will not be dishonored.

Who Should Disciple? All believers are commanded to disciple. Older women are specifically singled out and commanded to teach younger women.

Who Do We Disciple? Faithful women who possess genuine saving faith.

What Do We Teach to the Disciple? We teach them to be sober-minded, to love their husbands, to love their children, to be chaste or pure, to be keepers at home, to be good or benevolent, to be submissive to their own husbands, as well as the whole of Scripture.

When Do We Disciple? Every other week, every week, whenever.

Where Do We Disciple? Her home, your home, or wherever—be creative.

How Do We Disciple? By God's power, and with a lot of prayer and love.

My prayer for you is that you will desire to live a godly life in this ungodly age. And by doing so, I pray that you, yourselves, with the help of God, will be women who are sober-minded, who love your husbands and children, who are pure, who are keepers at home, who are good, and who are obedient to your own husbands. And then I trust you will take the challenge and pass it on to a younger woman! As John the Apostle said in 3 John 4, "I have no greater joy than to hear that my children walk in truth." I would add that there is no greater joy than to disciple young women and to watch them grow and walk in the truth!

About the Author

Susan Heck and her husband Doug have been married for 37 years. She has been involved in Women's Ministries for about 28 years. This included teaching Bible Studies, counseling, and leading Ladies with the Master women's ministry at Grace Community Church in Tulsa, Oklahoma (www.gccoftulsa.net).

Susan is a certified counselor with the National Association of Nouthetic Counselors (www.nanc.org). She is the author of "With the Master" Bible Study series for women. Previously published books in that series are,

With the Master in the School of Tested Faith:
A Ladies' Bible Study on the Book of James

With the Master on our Knees:
A Ladies' Bible Study on Prayer

With the Master In Fullness of Joy:
A Ladies' Bible Study on the Book of Phillipians

She is also the author of two published booklets: "Putting Off Life Dominating Sins" and "A Call to Scripture Memory." (Focus Publishing). Susan's teaching ministry is an outgrowth of her memorization work on the Bible. She has personally memorized 23 books of the New Testament word-for-word (The Gospel of Matthew, The Gospel of John, Romans, Second Corinthians, Galatians, Ephesians, Philippians, Colossians, First and Second Thessalonians, First and Second Timothy, Titus, Philemon, Hebrews, James, First and Second Peter, First, Second, and Third John, Jude, Revelation, one book of the Old Testament (Jonah), and several other portions of Scripture.

Susan and Doug have two grown children and seven grandchildren. Both children and their spouses are in full-time ministry. Because of the enthusiasm of ladies who have attended Susan's Bible studies, she has been invited to speak to a number of ladies groups both nationally and internationally (www.withthemaster.org).